DICTIONA

GW01044944

INDIAN

ENGLISH

V. Subhash

DICTIONARY OF INDIAN ENGLISH

FIRST EDITION

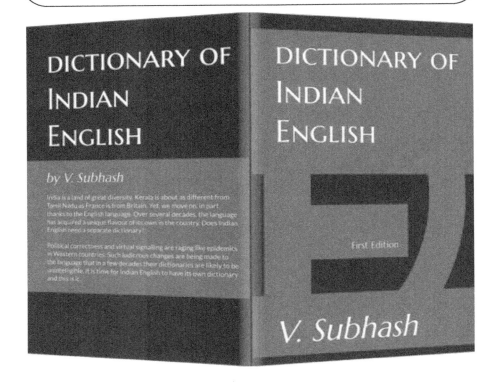

WRITTEN IN 2020 BY
V. Subhash

PRINTED AND PUBLISHED BY
V. Subhash
(www.VSubhash.in)

ISBN
978-93-5437-448-7 (Paperback)

CONTENTS

- Introduction
- Dictionary

- Books By V. Subhash

INTRODUCTION

India is a land of great diversity. Kerala is about as different from Tamil Nadu as France is from Britain. Yet, we move on, in part thanks to the English language. Over several decades, the language has acquired a unique flavour of its own in the country. People like to call it 'Indian English'; sometimes proudly and sometimes derisively. Indian English is of course not a different language. Yet, we often find that an Oxford or Webster's dictionary is inadequate or incorrect when dealing with certain words or phrases that have changed their meaning or purpose on the Indian soil. And, there are words that are unique to India, such as "prepone," which are not used anywhere else. In the first edition, this Dictionary of Indian English (DIE) hopes to provide a ready reference for such words and phrases. In a future edition, it will become a full-fledged dictionary. Its time is sure to come because of the fast-spreading pandemic of political correctness and mass stupidity.

A search-based version of this dictionary has been available for over a decade now on my website (**www.VSubhash.com** » **www.VSubhash.IN**). This book format has been created to provide:

- a different form of the dictionary that is accessible without an Internet connection and also
- as a stop-gap arrangement for a larger full-fledged dictionary in future when it will have over 55,000 words.

In its current form, this dictionary has over 400 words. For now, it is useful for

- non-Indian readers of Indian-English fiction
- foreign readers of Indian news
- foreign travellers to India

Notes:

- Several English words have originated from India. But, in the country of origin, these words are not very popular or have a different meaning. Therefore, the meanings provided by Western dictionaries for such words are wrong in the India context. In this dictionary, the generic Western definitions are marked as '(UK)' or '(US)', and the current Indian definition is marked as '(India)'.
- Some words such as 'untouchables' are only used by Westerners, particularly journalists, but not by Indians. Such terms are marked as '(politically incorrect)'.
- If you have any comments or suggestions, please mail them to **Info@VSubhash.Com**.
- The online version of this dictionary is available as a search engine in my free Android browser app - **Subhash Browser & RSS Feed Reader**. It is **the most feature-rich browser** there is for Android.

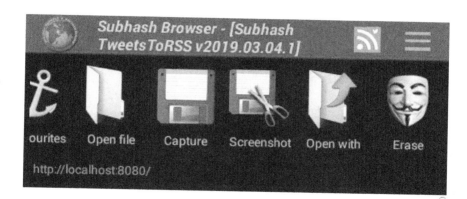

Subhash TweetsToRSS

Type @username/#hashtag/words to search:

#diy electronics

Examples @SubhashBrowser #GlobalCooling #gold price diy photo

Press to:

Generate RSS/HTML

☑ Include retweets

☐ Limit results to this location. (Choose)

Latitude 0.0

Longitude 0.0

DICTIONARY

A

aam aadmi: n. (Hindi) *common man* (similar to the British *man in the street* or the American *Average Joe*)

adalat: n. *justice; court*

agarbatti: n. *incense sticks*

   Plural: agarbattis; agarbathis

Agmark: n. Indian government *certification* or the *symbol* for food product quality

ahimsa: n. *non-violence*

air-dash: v. *rush* to a place by plane

almirah: (UK) *bureau*

alright: adj. (Colloquialism for) *all right*

amma: n. (Tamil/Malayalam) *mother*

anicut: n. *dam or water reservoir*

anti-social elements: *troublemakers; petty criminals; arsonists; looters*

   Synonym: *miscreants*

arranged marriage: n. *marriage* in which the prospective groom or bride is selected by parents/relatives

   See **love marriage**

ashram:
- *residence* of a **rishi/ godman**
- *organisation* run by a godman

   An *ashramite* is an inmate of an *ashram*.

auto: n. *autorickshaw*

avatar: n. *incarnation* of a god

ayah:
- n. *grandmother*
- n. *old maid*

B

Baapu: n. (Hindi) Mahatma Gandhi; *father*

Baba: n. (Title for) *holy man*

babu: n.

- (Hindi) *master; lord of the house*
- (UK) *government official*

plastic cover: n. plastic (shopping) bag

badla: n./adj. (Hindi) (getting) *something in return; revenge*

> In the stockmarkets, the *badla system* involves buying shares using borrowed money.

bahu: n.(Hindi) *daughter-in-law*

bandh: v. (Hindi) *mass shutdown* observed as a protest

> Rough translation: v. (Hindi) *stop*

bandobust: n. (Hindi) *protection* arranged and provided by police or other security personnel

banian: n. (Hindi) *vest*

bank holiday: *government or public holiday*

> Under the *Negotiable Instruments Act*, financial instruments remain valid for the next working day if the last date falls on a designated *bank holiday*

Basmati: n. (Hindi) special kind of *aromatic long rice* grown in India and Pakistan

> The colour of Basmati rice is a translucent, creamy white. Upon cooking, the rice grows twice as long but does not fatten much. The texture is firm and tender without splitting. It is also non-sticky. The aroma in Basmati arises from a cocktail of 100 compounds — hydrocarbons, alcohols, aldehydes and esters.

bata: n. (sometimes nominal) *special allowance* (paid for manual/casual labour or extra work)

batchmate: n. (Hindi) *someone who graduated with the same batch but not necessarily from the same class*

bazaar: n. *market*; *shop street*

benami: n./adj. (Hindi) *illegal property* or *illegally conducted transaction* in the name of another person, who acts a proxy for the real beneficiary, as defined by *The Benami Transaction (Prohibition) Act*

berth:

- n. *seat* in a sleeper compartment on a train where one can stretch completely flat to sleep

  > Only a *confirmed* reservation ticket is provided with a *berth*.
- *cabinet post* in the government

bhagwan: n. (Hindi) *god*

Many fraudulent **godmen** append *Bhagwan* to their names.

bhajan: *devotional song*

bhakti: n. *worship; devotion*

bidi: n. *tobacco rolled in tendu leaf* for smoking

> A bidi is used as a poor man's cigarette.

bike: n. *motorbike; motorcycle*

A bicycle is never referred as a 'bike'.

bits: n. *pieces of paper* used by students to cheat in examinations

blade: n. *safety razor*

Rarely refers to a knife.

board exams: n. (education) *finals examinations* for 10th or 12th standards conducted by State or Central government school education boards (administration)

bonnet: n. *hood* of car

bore: *bore well* dug for drinking water

brinjal: n. aubergine (British) or eggplant (American)

British Raj: *British colonial rule* in the Indian subcontinent

bund: Bank built around **anicut** to prevent water run-off or breach

bungalow:
- n. (India) *any big house*
- n. (UK) *independent house* with one upper floor

bunk:
- v. *skipping classes* (in school or college)

    Synonym: *cut* classes
- n. *fuel station*

bureau: n. tall *steel cabinet/cupboard*

bypoll: *mid-term elections*

C

capitation fees: *fees* charged by an educational institution over and above the approved fee structure (usually in the guise of a donation)

capsicum: n. *bell pepper* (the thick fleshy chilly)

casteism: n. *practice of caste system; caste politics*

Related: **communalism**

casteist party: n. *casteist party* that panders to a particular caste or group of castes.

Examples: BSP
Related: **communal party**

casual leave: *leave day from work*, not covered under designated leaves such as medical leave

Centre: *central government; Government of India; Union Cabinet*

chai: n. (Hindi) *tea*

challan: n. (Banking) *pay-in or remittance slip*

chalta hai: (Hindi) *it goes*

The typical Indian lackadaisical *it-will-do* or *anything-will-do* attitude is known as the *chalta hai* attitude.

chamcha: n. (Hindi) *sycophant*

chappals: n. (Footwear) *slippers*

Unlike in the West, slippers are used outdoors in India. Nobody wears footwear inside the house.

charpoy: *cot* with interwoven ropes to support the occupants

chats: *Indian snacks*

checkpost: n. (Hindi) *compulsory stop* on a road where transported goods are checked by the state government

Chief Secretary: *top bureaucrat* in a state government

chit: n. *financial scheme* in which a group of people contribute in a fixed amount every day/week/month and one of them gets to collect the entire amount by lucky draw each time

chowk: n. (Hindi) *market*

chowkidar: *watchman* or *caretaker*

churidar:
- (North India): *certain kind of garments* worn by men and women
- (South India): *North Indian-style garment* worn exclusively by females

cinema: n. (mistake) *feature film*

A cinema theatre is known as the theatre. The film is known as the cinema.

clean chit: n. *exoneration; acquittal; a not-guilty verdict*

Collector: n. *top bureaucrat* in a district administration

colony: *apartment complex*

As in *housing colony.*

communalism: n. *politics that openly favours one religion or divides society on religious lines*

Related: **casteism**

communal party: n. *political party that openly favours one religion or divides society on religious lines*

Examples: BJP
Related: **casteist party**

convent: *school* run by a Western Christian mission

cool bar: (South India) *stall* or *shop* selling soft drinks or fruit juices

The shop may identify itself as a *cool bar* but people will refer to it only as a *juice shop.*

country fellow: n. *country bumpkin*

country: pre. *traditional; rural and unsophisticated; made without licence or official sanction*

Example: A loaded .12-bore *countrymade* pistol was recovered from the **dacoit.**

cousin-brother: n. (mistake) *cousin*

creche: n. *kids daycare center*

crore: n. (Hindi) *1,00,00,000; 100 **lakh**s; 10 million*

A *crorepathi* is a person who is worth several crores of money.

cum: art. *and*

Examples: *seminar cum workshop; journey-cum-reservation ticket*

curd rice: n. (South India) *rice mixed/fried with curd*

Related: lemon rice; tamarind rice, coconut rice...

custodial death: *murder or alleged suicide* in police custody

cutting chai: n. (Bombay) *half a cup of tea*

D

dabba:

- n. *Punjabi restaurant*

    Synonym: *dhaba* In the South, Punjabi dhabas are open-air restaurants, usually found alongside highways. They are mainly patronised by truck drivers and North Indian travellers. The patrons are usually seated on **charpoys**.

- n. *box*

    Dabbawallahs are lunchbox couriers in Bombay who deliver home-made meals to workplaces shortly before lunchtime.

dacoit: n. *member of armed and mobile group of robbers*

dahi: n. (Hindi) *yoghurt*

dakshin: n. (Hindi) *South*

Uttar - North
Purab - East
Paschim - West

dal: n. *assembly; party; gram; lentils*

Related:

- channa dal - Bengal gram
- moong dal - green gram
- urad dal - black gram

dargah: n. *Muslim shrine; tomb of a Muslim saint*

darshan: n. (Hindi) *(visiting and) viewing* (usually of a deity in a temple)

Example: '*Party **high command** did not give darshan to the **dissidents**'*

Dearness Allowance: n. *cash payment* made to employees by an employer to offset the effects of inflation

departmental store: n. *self-service shop*

In most shops, customers give orders over the counter. They have no product aisles where the customers can walk in.

desi:

- adj. (Hindi) *local; Indian-made product*
- n. *citizen; Indian national*

Videsi would be *a foreigner* or *a foreign-made product*

dharma: n. (India) *religion; righteousness; philanthropy*

dhobiwallah: n. Washerman or laundryman (washes by hand rather than with a machine)

dhoti: n. (Hindi) *garment* composed of a white sheet used to cover the lower part of the body (from the hip to the ankles)

Related: mundu, veshti and lungi

dickey: n. *boot* of a car

disproportionate assets: n. *assets disproportionate to known sources of income; undeclared wealth*

dissidents: n. (Hindi) *sulking party leaders*

Dissidents usually are opposed to the current leadership and/or thinking about joining another party.

divas: (Hindi) n. *day; date*

Diwali: n. *festival of lights*

doubt: n. (mistake) question

Example: *I have some doubts in mathematics. Can you help me?*

dowry death: n. *suicide* by a married woman, prompted by her husband and/or in-laws who have been harassing her for more dowry

drumstick: n. (Hindi) *Mooringa olifera, a long narrow vegetable* that grows from a tree

dry grapes: n. *raisins*

durbar: n. (Hindi) *king's court*

E

elaichi: n. (Hindi) *cardamom*

electric trains: n. *trains* run by the Indian Railways in cities and suburban areas

The trains are pulled by electric locomotives and are officially called Electric Motor Units (EMUs).

Emergency: n. (Hindi) *suspension of the constitution* by Indira Gandhi in 1975, citing an *internal emergency* when the opposition parties made undemocratic attempts topple her democratically elected government

encounter: n. *extra-judicial killings* by police or paramilitary forces

The official story is the security personnel retaliated in self defence.

eve-teasing: n. *teasing or sexual harassment* of females, usually by **Roadside Romeos**.

> Tactics range from whistling, innuendoes, catcalls, singing, dancing, sign-making and sometimes even assault or murder.

eveninger: n. *evening newspaper*

eversilver: n. *stainless steel*

eyewash: n. *masquerade; coverup; pretense*

F

fair: adj. *light-skinned*

fancy store: n. (Tamil Nadu) *store* selling play items and things that help students perform their homework, assignments, and projects

feni: n. *liquor drink*, popular in Goa

> *Caju* is feni brewed from cashew. In Kerala, *toddy (kallu)* is a drink brewed from coconut shoots. In Tamil Nadu, *kallu* is brewed from palm tree. *Neera* is a very sweet non-alcoholic drink made from palm fruit. *Neera* naturally ferments into *kallu*. Related: **IMFL**

fidayeen: n. *Muslim suicide terrorist*

filter coffee: n. *drip-filtered coffee*

firang: adj. (Hindi) *foreign*

> A *firangi* is a foreigner.

fishcart: n. *tricycle* that has an attached cart for carrying goods

foreign hand: n. *involvement of a foreign spy agency* in a local incident

fundas: n. *fundamentals; essentials*

G

ganja: *dried hemp leaves* or the *resinous form of marijuana* prepared from flowering tops of the hemp plant

ghat:
- river bank
- steps alongside a river (meant for bathing rituals)
- cremation grounds
- mountain ranges along the east and west coasts of India i.e., Eastern Ghats and Western Ghats

ghee: n. (Hindi) *clarified butter*

gherao: n. (Hindi) *surrounding the offending party and raising slogans*

> Example: 'Striking workers *gheraoed* the management when the latter arrived at the factory'

gobar gas: n. (Hindi) *cooking gas* produced from a percolation tank collecting animal refuse

godman: n. *a man pretending to be a god or prophet of god on earth*

> Feminine: *godwoman*

godown: n. *warehouse*

good name: n. (Hindi) (literal) *shub naam*

> A respectful way asking a person's name is: "What is your good name?" Related: My name is *Subh*ash. It translates to *good language*. (The second part *bhash* means language.) Is it destiny that I write dictionaries?

goonda: n. (Hindi) *member of a crime gang; hired muscle; thug; troublemaker*

Government of India Undertaking: *company* owned by the Indian central government

grease: n.

- (India) *lubricating grease*
  > Never edible oil
- (US) *cooking fat*

gumastha: n. *clerk*

gunny bags: n. *bags* made from jute or hemp fibre

gur: n. (Hindi) *jaggery*

guru: n. (Hindi) *teacher; mentor; guiding philosopher; specialist in a field of activity*

gutka: v. (Hindi) *sweet flavoured tobacco product* that is chewed and then spat out

gyan: n. (Hindi) *knowledge; wisdom; thoughts; attention*

gymkhana: *public sports facility*

H

hafta: n. *bribe*

half ticket:

- n. *train ticket* issued to child passengers at half price
- n. *a small kid; an immature person.*

hall ticket: n. *admission slip issued to a student for a school/college examination*

handwash: n.

- place/convenience for washing hands
- act of washing hands
  > Most Indians wash their hands before eating because they eat with their

right hand (not with cutlery).

Harijans: n. (Sanskrit/politically correct) (literal) *Children of Hari* (Lord Krishna)

This politically correct term was given by Mahatma Gandhi to Scheduled Castes people to imply that they were also God's children. Many SC/ST groups opposed the use of this name and have preferred the use of the term *Dalits*, which is supposed to mean *depressed classes*.

havaldar: n. *policeman* whose rank falls between that of an inspector and constable

haveli: n. (North India) *private mansion*

hawala: n./adj. (Hindi/Urdu) *illegal system of remitting cash from abroad to India*

The hawala dealer accepts hard currency abroad and instructs an associate to deliver Indian rupees to a recipient living in India. No money passes through official channels. Since such transactions do not benefit the country's official foreign exchange reserves, they are banned under several legislations including the Benami Transactions Prohibition Act (1988) and Foreign Exchange Management Act (1999).

The reason for its popularity is because hawala dealers offer higher exchange rates and the transfer is done with very little delay or expense and leaves no paper trail. Hawala operations are closely allied with other illegal activities such as gold smuggling or drug trafficking.

The hawala dealer living abroad gets a good supply of hard currency with which he buys gold (or drugs or arms). He sends the contraband to his Indian associate who then sells it in India. The Indian associate uses the Indian currency he gets by selling the contraband and fulfills his commitments to make hawala payments to the individuals referred by the hawala dealer. The huge margins available in trading in currency and smuggling in contraband keeps the hawala operations in profit.

The hawala system is so efficient and so difficult to trace back that even foreign intelligence agencies like the Pakistani ISI use it to send funds to their collaborators in India. Investigative agencies are also extremely reluctant and/or unsuccessful in the prosecution of Hawala operators and beneficiaries.

hawaldar: n. (Hindi) *police constable*

head bath: n. (Tamil Nadu) *bath* that includes the washing the hair

As opposed to a bath that leaves the head dry or unwashed.
Related: **oil bath**

headweight: n. *proud and conceited*

high command: *top leadership* of a political party that controls all decisions

Example: *'Congress high command not in favour of fresh election in Goa.'*

hijra: n. (Literally) *eunuch*

This is a secretive hierarchical group in which the primary membership begins with a very crude form of castration. Even mildly effeminate men are coaxed into getting **castrated** when they join. This financially backward and discriminated community mostly survives by begging, entertainment and prostitution.

Hindi belt: n. Hindi-speaking states of *Bihar, Himachal Pradesh, Madhya Pradesh, Rajasthan, Uttar Pradesh, Uttarkhand and Uttaranchal*

Hinduism: n. There is no such thing as Hinduism. Contrary to what some say, it is not even a way of life. There is no common scripture or single deity to qualify as a religion, as exemplified by Christianity or Islam. There certainly was a Hindu civilization in the subcontinent for millennia and it continues to exist today. There are numerous Hindu castes that have some religion-like characteristics. Each Hindu caste is organized around an occupation and a deity. When Islam, Buddhism, Judaism, and Christianity were introduced through proselytization, the descendants of the converts were considered to belong to just another obscure caste. After the Revolt of 1857 against East India Company and the direct establishment of British rule in India, the British not only sought to keep Indians divided but also to reinforce the divisions. Hindu castes were then grouped under a 'Hindu religion' and other groups such as Muslims, Sikhs, Parsis and Christians were made separate from what was a common Indian civilization. (Christianity came to India before most European countries.) Even then, for many years afterwards, the words *Indian* and *Hindu* were synonymous.

Hindus: n. (Literally) *Indians; inhabitants of the lands adjoining the banks of river Sindh*. After the British started scripting and writing Indian history and particularly after the Revolt of 1857, this term has been used to refer to the majority community in India, as distinct from others such as Muslims and Sikhs.

Hindustan: n. (Literally) *land of Hindus*

> Like Bharath, this is another name for India. The term *Hindus* refers to all Indians. Before the British started writing Indian History, Indians of all denominations were referred as Hindus.

Hindustani:

- n. *Indian language* that is a mix of Hindi and Urdu
- n. *Indian*

Hindutva: n. *political strategy* followed by the Bharatiya Janata Party (BJP) and its allies for consolidating the 'Hindu vote bank'

Hinglish: n. *combination of Hindi and English*

history-sheeter: n. *person with a long criminal record*

Holi: n. (Literally) *festival of colours*

hooch: n. *illegally brewed liquor*

> A *hooch tragedy* occurs when industrial alcohol or carelessly distilled alcohol (which contains poisonous methanol) is consumed.

hotel: n. *restaurant* or *eatery*

> Not necessarily a place to stay

hukka: n. (Hindi) *tobacco smoking apparatus*, which forces the smoke to pass through a bowl of water before being inhaled

hundi: n. (Hindi) *donation collection box* in temples

hungama: n. (Hindi) *commotion; fuss; celebration; contest*

I

Iftar: n. *feast* arranged by Muslims to celebrate the end of the Ramzan month of fasting

Indian Acronyms and Abbreviations:

- AAI - Airport Authority of India
- AGP - Asom Gana Parishad
- AI - Air India
- AIADMK - All-India Anna Dravida Munnetra Kazhagam
- AIR - All India Radio
- AP - Andhra Pradesh; Arunachal Pradesh
- ASLV - Augmented Satellite Launch Vehicle
- BCCI - Board of Cricket Control in India
- BG - Broad Gauge (trains); Broad Guage railway tracks (5ft. 6in. the broadest in the world)
- BJP - Bharatiya Janata Party
- BSP - Bahujan Samaj Party
- CBI - Central Bureau of Investigation
- CBSE - Central Board of Secondary Education
- CII - Confederation fo Indian Industry
- CM - Chief Minister
- CPI - Communist Party of India
- CPI (M) - Communist Party of India (Marxist)
- CPI (ML) - Communist Party of India (Marxist-Leninist)
- CPWD - Central Public Works Department; PWD of the GOI
- DA - Dearness Allowance
- DD - DoorDarshan (state television)
- DK - Dravida Kazhagam
- DMK - Dravida Munnetra Kazhagam
- DoT - Department of Telecommunications
- DRDO - Defence Research and Development Organisation
- EMU - Electric Multiple Unit
- FC - Forward Caste
- FM - Finance Minister
- GoI - Government of India
- GSLV - Geostationary Launch Vehicle
- HC - High Court
- HP - Himachal Pradesh
- IA - Indian Airlines
- IAF - Indian Air Force
- IGNOU - Indira Gandhi National Open University
- IIM - Indian Institute of Management
- IIT - Indian Institute of Technology
- IMD - India Meteorological Department
- INSAT - Indian National Satellite
- IPKF - Indian Peace Keeping Force
- IRS - Indian Remote Sensing Satellite
- ISI - Formerly Indian Standards Institute, now renamed Bureau of Indian

Standards, thanks to Pakistan's intelligence agency Inter-Services Intelligence
- ISRO - Indian Space Research Organisation
- LoC - Line of Control (between Pakistan-Occupied Kashmir (POK) and Indian-controlled state of Jammu & Kashmir)
- Metre Guage - railway tracks (at 1 metre)
- MP - Madhya Pradesh
- NDA - National Democratic Alliance
- NIC : National Informatics Centre
- NRI - Non-Resident Indian
- NSC - National Savings Certificate
- OBC - Other Backward Classes
- ONGC - Oil and Natural Gas Commission
- PAN - Permanent Account Number (for income tax assessees)
- PF - Provident Fund
- PIL - Public Interest Litigation
- PMK - Pattali Munnetra Kazhagam
- PSLV - Polar Satellite Launch Vehicle
- PSU - Public Sector Unit
- PTI - Press Trust of India
- PWD - Public Works Department
- RAW - Research Samata Party
- SC - Scheduled Castes
- ST - Scheduled Tribes
- TN - Tamil Nadu
- ULFA - United Liberation Front of Asom
- UP - Uttar Pradesh
- VHP - Vishwa Hindu Parishad
- WB - West Bengal

Indianised place names

- Baroda - Vadodra
- Behar - Bihar
- Benares - Varanasi
- Bombay - Mumbai
- Calicut - Kozhikode
- Madras - Chennai
- Dilli - Delhi
- Calcutta - Kolkatta
- Laccadives - Lakshadweep
- Orissa - Odissa
- Pune - Poona
- Trichinopoly/Trichy - Tiruchirapalli/Tiruchi
- Trivandrum - Thiruvananthapuram

Indian-Made Foreign Liquor (IMFL): *traditional foreign alcoholic beverages made in India* (almost always made from bagasse)

Examples: whisky, brandy, beer, wine, gin, vodka, etc.
Traditional Indian liquor beverages like **toddy, feni**, etc., are considered to be *country* liquor. Shops that sell *country* liquor are known as *country* bars.

intimate: v. *inform*

    Example: 'You will be *INTIMATED* shortly.'

ISI Mark: A symbol of quality, certified by the *Bureau of Indian Standards* (BIS), which was formerly known as *Indian Standards Institute.*

item number: n. *song-dance sequence* in a movie featuring a glamorous actress, usually appearing in a cameo role

    The dancer/actress is known as the *item girl.*

J

jaggery: n. *unrefined coarse sugar*

    After the extraction of sugar, the remaining sugarcane syrup is concentrated by boiling. The residue collected from this process *jaggery*.

japti: n. (Hindi) *attachment of assets by court order*

jati: n. (Hindi)

* *caste* or *subcaste*
* *kind* or *type*

jawan: n. (Hindi) *soldier; youth*

jeevan: n. (Hindi) *life*

jehadis: *Muslim terrorists*

    Literally, a *jihadi* is someone involved in *jihad* or holy war.

jibbah: n. (South India) (Synonym for) *kurta*

    This is a collarless loose sometimes-knee-length shirt.

K

kabab: n. (Urdu) *skewered meat*

kaccha: n. *raw; unprepared; unsophisticated; low quality*

kajal: *kohl; eye liner*

    Indian kohl is not made from lead or antimony. It is made from the soot of a cotton wick soaked in a special combination of herbs, wood paste and oils.

kanjoos: n. (Hindi) *miser*

karma: n. (Hindi) *deeds; actions*

karyakartas: n. (Hindi) *workers*

khadi: n. *hand-woven cloth; goods made without the use of machines*

Supporters of Mahatma Gandhi's *Khadi* philosophy (in support of the village-based economy) buy products certified and sold by the *Khadi and Village Industries Commission* - **www.kvic.gov.in**.

Kharif: n. (Hindi) *autumn*

Related: **rabi**

kirana: n.

- *retail (or grocery) store*
- *Kirana*, the community whose hereditary profession is retail selling

kisan: n. (Hindi) *farmer*

kitty party: n. *a meeting of women* where chits are arranged or gossip is exchanged

Kollywood: n. *Kodambakkam film industry* in Chennai, Tamil Nadu, where a lot of South Indian movies (Tamil, Malayalam, Telugu and Kannada) are produced

Related: **Tollywood**

kurta: n. (Hindi) *loose shirt*

kuruvai: n. (Tamil Nadu) *a short-term crop season* from June to July

Related: **samba**

L

ladies seat: n. *seat reserved for ladies* in a bus

A *ladies compartment* is a train compartment reserved for ladies. A *ladies special* is a bus reserved for women. A *lady doctor* or a *ladies specialist* is an obstetrcian-gynecologist.

ladiesfinger: n. *okra*

Synonym: *Ladies' finger*

lakh: n. (Hindi) *1,00,000; 100 thousands; 1/100* **crore**

langurs: n. (Hindi) *monkeys*

lathi: n. *long bamboo stick* used by policemen to strike blows

lathicharge: n. *an assault by policemen using lathis*

laxman rekha: n. (Hindi) *limit; border; threshold*

Origin: Lord Ram, his wife Sita and brother Laxman were living in exile in the forest. A demoness named Surpanaka wanted to marry Ram but he remained devoted to his wife. She tried to lure Laxman but he chopped off her nose. An enraged Surpanaka complained to her brother Ravan, the King of Lanka (Sri Lanka). They plotted together to extract revenge. Surpanaka disguised herself as a deer and enchanted Sita. Sita asked Ram to capture the deer. Ram disappeared into the forest in search of the deer and did not return even after a long time. An anxious Sita asked Laxman to go in search of Ram. Suspicious of the deer story, Laxman drew a line around their house with a magical arrow and asked Sita to stay behind it.

When Laxman left the house, Surpanaka's brother Ravana tried to capture Sita. However, the line drawn by Laxman, the *Laxman Rekha* burned him. (Think of it like a a protective force field.) He then tricked Sita into crosssing the *Laxman Rekha* and he kidnapped her to Lanka.

This and how Ram rescues Sita is the story of the famous epic *Ramayana*. If Sita had not crossed the *Laxman Rekha*, there would have been no Ramayana. When the US president talks about a 'red line' that should not be crossed, he is talking about a *Laxman Rekha*.

Related: **nose cut**

leela: n. (Hindi) *tale; romance*

LIC policy: n. (euphemism) a *life insurance policy*

Life insurance was synonymous with the Life Insurance Corporation (LIC) of India (a **Government of India Undertaking**) for several decades.

License Raj: *most of independent India's history* when much of internal economy was controlled by the state

Synonym: *Licence-Quota-Octoroi Raj*
Indian businessmen used to complain that the **British Raj** was replaced by the *License Raj*.

load shedding: *practice of decreasing the voltage or cutting the supply of electricity altogether* to limit consumption or handle limited supply

log: n. (Hindi) *people; citizens*

Lok Adalat: n. *mobile judiciary panel* that provides speedy justice

Accompanied by local administration officials, the panel visits villages and towns, and tries to find amicable solutions to settle local disputes.

love marriage: n. *marriage that follows a love affair*, as opposed to an **arranged marriage**

M

Maha: adj. (Hindi) *big; great*

maida: n. *maize (corn) flour*

maidan: n. (Urdu) *playground; stadium*

management seats: *student vacancies* in a private educational institution that are offered by the management using its own discretion and/or at a higher fee structure than *reserved seats*

mandi: n. (Hindi) *market*

mantra: n. (Hindi) *magic; ritualistic chants; slogan; guiding philosophy*

mantri: n. (Hindi) *minister*

Manu: Pr. n. (Hindi/Sanskrit) *first Indian lawgiver*

Manu is the author of *Manusmriti*. It outlines the Indian caste system.

medicos: *medical students or doctors*

mehndi: henna; the art applying henna paste on the skin and creating the design

mela: n. festival

Example: Indian Bank will conduct a loan *mela* for new home owners.

memsahib: n. (Hindi) *wife of the master*

militants: n. euphemism for *terrorists*

military hotel: n. *hotel that serves non-vegetarian food* because all soldiers are assumed to eat meat

minority community: n. (euphemism) *Muslims*

> Though there are plenty of other minority communities such as Sikhs, Jains and Christians, the term *minority community* was used by the Indian government for decades exclusively to refer to Muslims.

mixie: n. *electric blender or mixer-grinder* used in kitchens

mofussil areas: n. (Urdu) *outlying districts; areas away from the district capital*

mohajir: n. (Urdu) *refugee.*

> In Pakistan, the term *Mohajirs* refers to Indian Muslims who moved to Pakistan around the time of the Partition.

mohalla: n. (Urdu) *Muslim locality or neighbourhood*

moral responsibility: n. (politics) usually accompanied by a demand for resignation

morcha: n. (Hindi) *protest campaign*

mufti: adj. *plainclothes* or *civilian dress*

muhurtam: n. *auspicious time for marriages*, as per Hindu calendar

mundu: n. (Malayalam) *white dhoti*

munsif: n. (Urdu) *low-level judge*

mutt: n. (Tamil) *religious and monastic institution*

> Synonyms: *madam; matam; math*
> Examples: *Sri Ahobila Matam; Kanchi Mutt; Shri Ramakrishna Math*

N

naik: n. *non-commissioned officer* in the Indian Army

nariyal: n. (Hindi) *coconut*

national integration: n. *unity in diversity*

> This refers to the aspiration of achieving cohesive unity despite the country's unsurpassed level of diversity.

native place: n. *wherever one came from* before moving to the current location

naxalites n. *terrorists* with a Communist excuse

naya: adj. (Hindi) *new*

near and dear: n. *friends and family*

needful: n. *whatever is required or needs to be done,* as demanded by the circumstances

> Example: '*The Handloom Board should understand the plight of weavers. It should do the needful and justify its existence.*'
>
> The word needful is used as a noun and not as an adjective. With this usage, the word is always accompanied with the article *the*.

neta: n. (Hindi) *politician*

North Block: *office block* housing the Ministry of Finance and the Ministry of Home Affairs

> Related: **South Block**

North-East: The neglected and mismanaged North-Eastern states of India - Assam, Nagaland, Tripura, Meghalaya, Manipur, Mizoram and Arunachal Pradesh.

> Also known as *Seven Sisters of the North-East*. The North-East shares international borders China, Tibet, Bhutan, Bangladesh, and Myanmar (Burma).

nose cut: n. (Tamil Nadu) *a sharp retort or insult*

> Related: **Laxman Rekha**

NRIs: *Non-Resident Indians*

> NRI has special meaning under the Indian Income Tax Act: *an individual being a citizen of India or a person of Indian origin, who is not ordinarily resident.*

nullah: n. (Hindi) *stream; watercourse*

O

official machinery: *government infrastructure; government facilities*

oil bath: n. (Tamil Nadu) *bath* taken after applying oil all over the body

> Related: **head bath**

open quota: *seats in educational institutions or job vacancies in government organisations* that are not reserved for any particular community

opticals: n. *shop selling eye glasses*

other backward classes: *OBCs; castes recognised by the Indian constitution and state-laws as below FC (forward castes or upper castes) and above SC/ST (Scheduled Castes/Scheduled Tribes)*

P

Pak: abbrv. Pakistan

Example: 'Prime Minister blames Pak groups for terrorist attack'

pan: n. (Hindi) *preparation* made from betel leaf, areca nuts, lime and some other ingredients

panchayat: n. (Hindi) *village council*

paneer: n. (Hindi) *fresh delicate cheese or milky cheese* rich in nutrients and made from low fat milk

paper leak: n. *release of unauthorised copies of question papers,* prior to an examination

parallel cinema: *art films*

pariah: n. (UK) *outcast*

Similar to 'untouchables', use of this term is offensive to people belonging to Scheduled Caste/Tribe communities.

parlour: n. *beauty parlour* for ladies

Partition: The partition of the Indian Subcontinent in 1947 leading to the formation of the separate states of India and Pakistan.

passed out: v.

- (India) (mistake) *secured a pass* (in an examination)
- (UK) *became unconscious; expel in stools*

patta: n. *documents; title*

Patta lands have a clear title of ownership as opposed to *poromboke* land. Poromboke lands have no owners and by default belong to the government.

phenyl: n. *bathroom/toilet disinfectant*

Synonyms: phenol, phenol, phenoyl, phenoil, phenyle

PIL: abbrv. *Public Interest Litigation*

This is a lawsuit filed in the interest of the public by a citizen who is not directly affected by the defendants mentioned in the suit.

PIN code: n. six-digit *Postal Index Number*

Similar to the US ZIP codes, every Indian town or city or locality can be reached by this postal code.

pooja: n. (Hindi) *worship; worship ritual*

prepaid: n. *mobile telephone connection for which payment has to be made ahead of consuming the service*

For a *postpaid* connection, the bill is paid after a month of usage. *Prepaid recharge* is the payment of the service charge for **talktime** the prepaid connection.

prepone: v. *to reschedule an event or activity ahead of when it was originally scheduled*

President's rule: *supercession of a state government* by the central government under Article 356 of the Indian constitution

pseudosecular: *parties allegedly partial to Muslims while claiming to be secular*

This is an allegation that BJP charges the INC with.

pucca: n. (Hindi) *genuine; good; sophisticated; good quality*

Antonym: kutcha
A *pucca road* is a black-topped road. A dirt road is a kachcha road. A *pucca house* is one made of brick and cement. A thatch shed is a*kutcha* structure.

purana:

- (adjective) old
- history
- (Capitalized noun) Record of events that are believed to have occurred long ago. The Puraanas are also considered as the recorded history of Bharat (India). There are eighteen Puraanas. They are written in the form of dialogue, between a scholar and an inquirer. The subject of the Puraanas is: the genealogies of kings, the reigns of kings, ruling dynasties. The 18 Puraanas are:
  - Vishnupurana
  - Matsyapurana
  - Kurmapurana
  - Varahaparana
  - Vamanapurana
  - Bhagwatpurana
  - Naradiyapurana
  - Garudapurana
  - Padmapurana
  - Lingapurana
  - Shivapurana
  - Skandapurana
  - Agnipurana
  - Brahmapurana
  - Brahmandapurana
  - Brahmavivartapurana
  - Markandevapurana
  - Bhavishyapurana

purdah: n. (Hindi) *veil; Muslim code of dress for women*

pyjama: n. (Hindi) *loose shirts and pants* worn by men in North India

Not necessarily bedtime clothes

Q

qila: n. (Hindi) *fort*

The *Red Fort*, location of the *Republic Day* parade, is known as *Lal Qila*.

R

Rabi: n. (Hindi) *spring*

    Related: **kharif**

Raj: n.

- (India) *king; kingdom; lord; reign*
- (UK) *British colonial rule or empire in the Indian subcontinent*

Raja: n. (Hindi) *king*

ration shops: adj. (Hindi) *shops selling rationed goods* supplied by the government via the Public Distribution System (PDS) for the benefit of lower-income families

regional aspirations: *regional political demands* unmet because they are trapped within a larger state or having no influence in the central government

regularise: v. (Hindi) *legally legitimise* illegal (constructions, house plans, etc.)

reservation: n.

- *policy of reserving jobs and seats in educational institutions for certain communities such as the SC/ST*
- *advance booking of tickets in trains and buses*

    Tatkal reservation is out-of-turn train ticket reservation for emergency reasons.

rest house: n. *fully furnished accommodation meant for travellers*

    Rest houses are usually built by the government. Americans Beware! A *rest house* is not a *restroom* (toilet).

resume: n. (mistake) *biodata; professional profile; curriculum vitæ*

    Written as résumé and pronounced as *ray-soo-may*

revert: v. (mistake) *reply* (to a letter, email or missed phone call)

    Example: '*I will revert to your query later in this message*'

rickshaw: n.

- (obsolete) (manually-pulled) *cycle rickshaw*
- *auto rickshaw*

    Synonym: **auto**

rishi: n. (In ancient times or mythology) *sage or mendicant*

road roko: n. (literal) *protest stopping road traffic*

    Synonym: *rasto roko*
    Rail rokos are intended to stop rail traffic.

roadside Romeos: n. *Male youth* who harass girls, usually in and around areas such as bus-stops, temples and colleges, etc.

    Related: **eve-teasing**

roti: n. (Hindi) *form of unleavened bread made from wheat*

    Political euphemism for *khana* (food), as in *roti, kapda aur makan* (food, clothes and shelter).

rowdy: n. *criminal; thug* in the employ of criminals

Plural: *rowdies*

A rowdy with a long criminal record is known as **history-sheeter**.

rubber: n. *eraser*

ryots: n. (Urdu) *farmers*

S

sabha: n. *cultural association; political assembly or conference*

sadhu: n.

- (Hindi): *ascetic*
- (Tamil): *timid or harmless person*

samadhi: n. *death; grave*

> Several ascetics in the past have wilfully initiated death after sitting in meditation. That is a *samadhi*. Today, followers of any two-bit politician can designate his grave as a *samadhi*.

samba: n. (Tamil) the *main crop season* beginning in August

> Related: **kuruvai**

sanyas: n. *ascetic life*

> Synonym: *sanyasa*
> A *sanyasi* (Fem. *sanyasini*) or *sadhvi* is a person who has taken up *sanyas*.

Sardarji: n. *an elderly Sikh male*

> A Sikh female is known as a *Sardarni*.

sari: n. (Hindi) *strip of cloth*, usually about 6 yards in length, worn as a garment by women

> It is worn over a *choli* (blouse) and *ghagra* (petticoat) or *lehenga* (long skirt).

sarkar: adj. (Hindi) *government*

Scheduled Castes: (politically correct) *castes that traditionally occupied the lowest strata of the Indian caste hierarchy*

Scheduled Tribes: (politically correct) *communities that have traditionally lived in forested areas, subsisting on forest produce* as hunters or gatherers

> Synonym: Adivasi (first residents); *tribals*

seat-sharing: *political arrangement* enabling a larger party gain the support of a smaller party in an election by conceding a number of election seats to the latter

seva: n. (Hindi) *service; help*

shakehand: n. (mistake) gesture of *shaking hands*

> Example: *The teacher gave me a shakehand.*

shakti: n. *power; energy; strength*

shamiana: n. (Urdu) *tent*

shanti: n. (Hindi) *peace; silence*

sindoor: n. (Hindi) *vermilion* paste or powder, usually applied as a dot or a mark (*tilak*) on the forehead.

  The sticker version of *sindoor* used by women is called *bindi*.

sleeper: *train compartment* that has seats on which passengers can lie down to sleep_

sloka: *Sanskrit verse or prayer* meant to be chanted aloud or meditated upon

social justice: (euphemism) *social empowerment of SC/ST*

South Block: n. *office block* housing the Prime Minister's Office (PMO), Ministry of Defence and the Ministry of External Affairs

  The South Block is one of two secretariat blocks. The other is known as **North Block**.

speak in English: (mistake) *speak English*

speed-breaker: n. *road bump*

Sri: *decorative title for men*

  Synonyms: *Sree; Shree; Shri*
  Feminine: *Sreemati; Shreemathi; Shrimati*

standard: n. (education) *school grade or academic year*

supari killer: n. *hired killer*

  Supari is the contract.

Swadeshi: adj./n. (Hindi) *a movement or determination to by* **desi** *goods*

swami: n. (Hindi) *God; godman*

Syrian Christians: n. *Malayali Christians*

  They do not include Catholic Syrians or Roman Catholics. Syrian Christians claim to be followers of St. Thomas.

T

tainted: adj. (politics) *tainted* politician has one or more pending criminal case(s) against his/her name.

talktime: n. *cumulative phone call duration*, measured in minutes, that has been purchased for **prepaid** mobile phone connection

tamasha: n. (Hindi) *joke; drama; pointless activity*

  Khel is a *game*. Politics is sometimes described as having become a *khel* or *tamasha*.

Tamizh: n. (synonym) *Tamil*

  A *Tamizhan* is a *Tamilian*

tanda: v. (Hindi) *cold*

tandoori: adj. (Hindi) *North-Indian style of cooking*

The food is cooked in a hearth over hot coals.

tantric: n. (Hindi) *wizard; magician*

Tantra is a *trick.*

tehsildar: n. (Urdu) *Revenue Department official* in charge of a *tehsil* or a *taluk* (a revenue district)

Synonym: *tahsildar*

tempo: n. *three-wheeled cargo transport vehicle*

tender coconut: n. (Tamil) coconut water

Origin: Tamil word *ilaneer*, whose literal translation is *young coconut*

thali:
- (North India) *plate; meal*
- (South India) *wedding thread/necklace (mangalsutra)*

thana: n. (Hindi) *police station*

third front: *coalition* of political parties attempting an alternate political choice, which does not include the ruling party nor the main opposition party

tiffin: *light morning meal*

A *tiffin carrier* or *tiffin pack* is a lunch box.

timepass:
- v. *wasting time away*
- n. *hobby*

tolet: n. *to let*

'Tolet' boards are signs announcing vacant accommodation.

Tollywood: n. *Tollygunge (Kolkatta) film industry*, which produces mainly Bangla movies

Reated: **Kollywood**

too good: (mistake) *very good*

Example: *This movie is too good.*

tortoise coil: n. *mosquito-repellant coils*

Origin: The once-popular Tortoise coils were originally made from a mixture of herb extracts. They drove away mosquitoes but were made obsolete by allethrin-based mosquito repellants, which actually killed the mosquitoes.

U

Udipi hotel: *hotel* run by Brahmin from the town of Udipi or specialising in Udipi-style of South-Indian cooking

ulta: adj. (Hindi) *upside-down; opposite*

undertrial: n. *jailed inmate* who is awaiting trial or whose trial is currently underway

Untouchables: (politically incorrect) *Scheduled Castes/Tribes*

updation: n. *updating*

> Example: *'Write a program for creation, deletion and updation of database records.'*

upgradation n. *upgrade; process of applying or effecting an upgrade*

utsav: n. (Hindi) *festival*

> Synonym: *mela*
> A *mahotsav* is a big festival.

V

vaastu: n. (Hindi) the *ancient Indian tradition of constructing buildings*

> Learn more about *Vastu* using **my book**.

VCD: n. *video compact disc*

> VCDs are regular compact discs (CD-ROMs) but contain videos in MPEG-1 format. To play VCDs on a PC, use the freeware software **Subhash VCDPlayer** (Windows 9x/Me/2000/XP/7/Vista/7/8). One VCD holds 81 minutes of video so a typical Indian movie comes in a case of two VCDs.

veg: abbrv. *vegetarian*

> *Non-veg* is the abbreviation of *non-vegetarian*.
>
> Examples:
> - I hate *veg* food.
> - This is a *non-veg* hotel.

veshti: n. (Tamil) *white dhoti.*

A dhoti with coloured patterns or designs is called a *lungi*. Unlike veshtis, lungis are not considered as formal wear.

vote bank: *votes of a particular community* that is expected to vote *en masse* in favour of a political party or alliance.

Traditionally, Muslims have been voting *en masse* and political parties have been offering all kinds of sops and incentives to win their support.

Tired of accusing these parties of playing 'vote bank politics' and practicing pseudosecularism, the Sangh Parivar went ahead with its own brand of vote-bank politics known as *Hindutva*. And, it has had considerable success in combating once unassailable influence of the 'Muslim vote bank.'

W

wallah:

- masc. n. (Hindi) *person.*

  Feminine: *wali.*

- sfx. (Hindi) *tradesman.*

  Examples: *doodhwallah* (milkman), *chaiwallah* (tea seller) and *dhobiwallah* (laundryman).

- sfx. (Parsi) -*wala.*

  A *Mr. Biscuitwala* might be involved in biscuit trade or may have had a ancestor who was.

wet grinder: n. (South India) *kitchen appliance* used to grind wet grain or pulses.

It creates a wet paste, rather than a powdery flour. It is necessary to make South-Indian tiffin staples such as *idli, dosas* and *vadais.*

wheatish complexion: adj. (classified advertisements) *neither dark-skinned nor light-skinned*

Y

yagna: n. *Vedic ritual* performed by priests

yatra: n. (Hindi) *journey; travel*

A *yatri* is a traveller. A *yatri nivas* is a travellers' lodge. A *padayatra* or *padyatra* is a journey/pilgrimage on foot. A *rath yatra* is a travel on a *rath* (chariot). BJP leader L. K. Advani pioneered the use of *rath yatras* for political purposes.

Z

zamindar: n. (Hindi) *rich man* (in colonial times) with large land holdings.
 Plural: zamindars, zameendars

Well, you have finished the book. If you give it a good rating (☆ ☆ ☆ ☆ ☆) or review online, it would be much appreciated. If you have any corrections or suggestions, write to me at **Info@VSubhash.Com**.

Some of my titles are available for FREE on several ebook stores and library apps. Give them a try. I have written more than two dozen non-fiction books on a wide range of subjects. I have also written ONE fiction title(s)! Check the backlist for more details or visit: **www.VSubhash.IN/books.html**

Books By V. Subhash

I invite you to visit my site **WWW.VSUBHASH.IN**, and check out my other books, special discounts, sample PDFs and full ebooks. In 2020, I started publishing books. For two decades before that, I have been publishing feature articles, free ebooks (old editions still available), software (server/desktop/mobile), reviews (books, films, music and travel), funny memes and cartoons. You can follow these adventures on my blog: **http://www.vsubhash.in/blogs/blog/index.html**

My books for children are under the pseudonym **Ólafía L. Óla** (because it has laugh and LOL).

  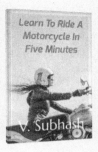 

   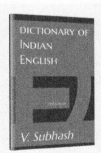

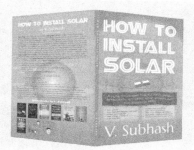

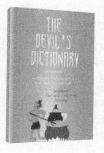

About the author

V. Subhash is an invisible Indian writer, programmer and cartoonist. In 2020, he published one of the biggest jokebooks of all time and then followed it up with a tech book on FFmpeg and a 400-page volume of 149 political cartoons. Although he had published a few ebooks as early as 2003, Subhash did not publish books in the traditional sense until 2020. For over two decades, Subhash had used his website **www.VSubhash.com** as the main outlet for his writing. During this time, he had accumulated a lot of published and unpublished material. This content and the automated book-production process that he had developed helped him publish 21 books in his first year. In February 2023, Apress (SpringerNature) published his rewritten and updated FFmpeg book as *QUICK START GUIDE TO FFMPEG*. Thus, by early 2023, Subhash had published 30 books! In 2022, Subhash ran out of non-fiction material and tried his hand at fiction. The result was *UNLIKELY STORIES*, a collection of horror and comedy short stories. After adding new stories to this fiction title (for its second edition), Subhash plans to pause his writing and move on to other things. Subhash pursues numerous hobbies and interests, several of which have become the subject of his books such as *COOL ELECTRONIC PROJECTS*, *HOW TO INSTALL SOLAR* and *HOW TO INVEST IN STOCKS*. He was inspired to write his jokebook after years of listening to vintage American radio shows such as *Fibber & Molly* and *Duffy's Tavern*.